THE VOICE OF HOPE

Jessica's Corner

Jessica Roman

Copyright © 2013

Literacy-in-Motion

Jessica Roman

All rights reserved. No portion of this book may be reproduced, scanned, stored in a retrieval system, transmitted in any form or by any means - electronically, mechanically, photocopy, recording, or any other - except for brief quotations in printed reviews, without written permission of the publisher. Please do not participate in or encourage piracy of copyrighted materials in violation of the author's rights. Purchase only authorized editions. All scripture quotations are taken from the King James Version (KJV) of the Holy Bible.

1. Library of Congress Cataloging-in-Publication Data
2. All scriptures referenced throughout this book have been quoted from the King James Version Bible. All biographical accounts referenced throughout this book are that of the author, Jessica Roman.

ISBN: 978-0-578-13571-7

1. Christian - Religious Life. Printed in the United States of America

Published by

Literacy in Motion, LLC

6212 US Hwy 6, Suite 232, Portage IN 46368

www.LiteracyinMotion.com

The Voice of Hope

Jessica Roman

Dedication

First and foremost, I must give all glory to God for He is the head of my life. Next, I'd like to thank my awesome Pastors, Dierre and Patricia Glenn of Advancing Christ Kingdom Ministries. You inspired me to discover God-given gift within me.

Last, but certainly not least, I'd like to thank my amazing family. Grandma, thank you for being steadfast through life's ups and downs. Your constant encouragement has inspired me to achieve things I never dreamed possible. To my 3 wonderful and beautiful boys Eddie Jr., Alex, and Donavan, Mommy loves you so much. To my loving Husband, thank you for standing beside me all these years. I love you so much Care Bear. You're my heart and I truly thank God for you!

"As for me and my house, we will serve the Lord."
Joshua 24:15

"Dream Until Your Dreams Come True"

TABLE OF CONTENT

PREFACE
JESSICA ROMAN   13

CHAPTER 1   JANUARY
THE NEW YOU: YOUR SALVATION   15

CHAPTER 2   FEBRUARY
LETTING GO/MOVING FORWARD   21

CHAPTER 3   MARCH
OBEDIENCE IN GOD   27

CHAPTER 4   APRIL
FORGIVENESS   31

CHAPTER 5   MAY
LOVE   35

CHAPTER 6   JUNE
PRAYER   39

CHAPTER 7   JULY

MARRIAGE   43

CHAPTER 8   AUGUST

CHOSEN   49

CHAPTER 9   SEPTEMBER

TEMPTATION   53

CHAPTER 10 OCTOBER

WHICH WILL YOU CHOSE? HEAVEN OR HELL   57

CHAPTER 11 NOVEMBER

GIVING THANKS HELPING OTHERS   61

CHAPTER 12 DECEMBER

REASON FOR THE SEASON   65

Preface
By Jessica Roman

I dedicated my life to Christ in March of 2010. Since receiving Jesus as my Lord and Savior, life has never been the same. When going through the pitfalls of purposeless living, you may find yourself asking, "why me?" But, despite life's trails, tribulations, and failures, God can turn your failures into fruitfulness. Don't allow the negative voices from without and within to disqualify you from God's design. Instead, we should be saying, "why not me?" I want to encourage you to never give up. Always believe.

I started an inspirational FaceBook page named ***Jessica's Corner*** that touches people all over the world. I was inspired to turn it into a book to continue to touch others. I encourage you to keep God first and trust Him always. He can make the impossible possible!

January

Chapter 1
The New You: Your Salvation

Welcome to the new you. We usually say Happy New Year; well, I am here to say, "Happy New You!" When you align your plans with God's purpose for your life, great things are destined to happen. This is a new beginning God has given to you. Accepting Christ as Lord and Savior is the greatest decision of your life. I pray many blessings over you.

God will show you things you never could imagine. Show people the new you. What you speak is what you must learn to live. When you change, many will watch to see if you are living the life you profess. You may be the only bible someone else sees. They will watch you so you must lead by example. You will no longer be a follower but a leader. For this you will be a blessing to God and you will bring others to him. Share your gift with the world and don't be ashamed of who you are or who God says you are. You are who you are by the Grace of God.

I came up with this saying that I often use to encourage myself:

> "I am who I am and it will never change. I will continue to walk, talk, and live for God! Accept me or turn away; but I forever will remain the same. A

child of God is who I will remain."

I love this because it is saying that no matter who you are, if you can't accept who I am then they can just walk away. You will learn by experience, that in this change, you will lose people along the way. Some friends and family, but that is okay. With God you can do all things, and don't you know there is more to gain than lose.

> *2nd Corinthians 5:17*
>
> *"Therefore if any man be in Christ, he is a new creature: old things are passed away; behold, all things are become new."*

FRESH MINDSET

Today, make the decision to let go of all the negative people, places, and things that have held you back. Don't let yesterday's worries enter today's new beginning. God has greater things in store for you.

ATTITUDE

We must not let the worldly influences affect our attitude and allow temporary feelings to dictate life changing decision. God is greater. We must not let what others say affect us and force us to fall back. Believe and trust what God says about you. As Believers, we must learn to lean on God. Men fail. God never fails.

When times get hard, you may feel like no one is around to help. Rest assured that God has not given up on you. We must keep the faith when we are going through storms of life. Tests and trials will come even though you are saved. It will not be easy. We, as Christians, will go through more just because of who we are. The enemy will test and tempt you. During these times of hardships, don't allow yourself to give up. Stand on the Word of God and trust in Him to see you through.

I wanted to give up a lot in the past. I questioned myself over and over again whether life was worth living. God has revealed many things to me since I have been saved. He blessed me with that which the world could never give me. God is truth, love, and forgiveness. The world is full of dishonesty, lies, hurt, and pain. However, God has shown me so much love and happiness during hard times. I will stand strong as a Christian because Earth is temporary. Heaven is eternal. Heaven is a place of love, truth, freedom, laughter, and happiness absent of tears and worries. One day, I will be reunited with those I have lost and be with my true father. Your reward is eternal life.

February

Chapter 2

Letting Go/Moving Forward

Baggage (Letting Go and Letting God)

While letting go of the past is difficult to discuss, it is easy to remember because it's what we know. The hurt, pain, and heartache are often all we remember in life. You must trust in Him to see you through the difficult times and take you beyond painful memories. To move forward, we must not step back into what God has delivered us from. The past is always going to be there, that's why it's called the past.

God wants you to create a brand new start. Don't allow the enemy to keep you stuck. Allow God to pull you up and out of your comfort zone. The enemy wants you to stay comfortable, but God wants you to grow and move forward. Letting go sounds hard, and sometimes it is, but when you really cast your care to God, it becomes easier. You must really be willing to "let it go" and let God take control. When you really let go, you forget and not allow the enemy to keep reminding you of your past.

Stay focused on God and allow Him to work the things out for you. Do not allow the enemy to keep you where he wants you to be. Allow God to create a new way of thinking and a new outlook on life. That's when you will see the work of God manifesting in your life. Letting go is difficult; however, when you let go and give it to God, He makes it easier.

God always makes a way as long as you believe, trust, and stay faithful in Him. God will always stay faithful to you. Today, whatever it is, I ask you to let go and let God. Your life is worth so much more. This world is temporary, but your life after this place is eternal.

"Live your life through the eyes of a child, for no matter the situation, they keep smiling and playing."

Reason for the Season of Letting Go

Do you find yourself having trouble letting go of a past relationship, a hurt from a friend, family member, or even the death of a loved one? Not everyone is meant to be in your life forever. Some are there just a season. God places people in our lives for a season to help us grow.

When the season comes to an end with a person, place, or thing, we must not allow ourselves to chase after what God is purging. This can and will stop your spiritual growth. We must learn how to release old things for the new things to fall into place. Pray and allow God to lead you. Read the Word daily, meditate in prayer, and watch as things around you start to change.

Now, this is not easy. It will take time, so you must stay positive and trust God to see it through. In time, it will be so easy that you will no longer allow it to affect you. Remember, God can do all things; just continue to keep your eyes on God and watch things change around you and for you. Stay encouraged. Remain faithful in God, and he will remain faithful in you.

I have come up with a few steps in order to help you let go and move forward. It takes time to let go of things that hurt, but it is necessary in order to grow as a Christian.

Step one: Pray

Allow God to take it from you. Do not allow the enemy to come in and remind you of the past. You can't move forward if you keep looking back. God wants you to enjoy life and not dwell on what was. When someone hurt you, and it's over with, don't allow yourself to remain hurt. Often times, the person who hurt you has moved on and doesn't continue to think about it. They are not losing sleep, so why should you. Let it go and allow God to move you forward. Keep God first, and take Him wherever you go. If He can't go, don't you!

Step two: Forget

After you have prayed, you must forget. Don't allow hurt to occupy space in your mind. Allow yourself to say, "What was done is finished, and it is my time to move forward." Do not let the enemy keep you bound to what God has delivered you from. When God says it's time to let go, we must obey.

March

Chapter 3

Obedience in God

We demonstrate our love for God by our obedience to his Word. As stated in John 14:15 & 21, "He who has my commandments and keeps them, it is he who loves me," "And he who loves me will be loved by my father, and I will love him and manifest myself to him." Did you notice the blessings promised to those who love him and keep his commandments? If we love him, the Father will love us, and he will love us and manifest himself to us.

Later in his life, John connected the concepts of love for God and obedience. As stated in I John 2:3-6, "Now by this we know that we know Him, if he keep His commandments. He who says, "I know Him," and does not keep his commandments, is a liar, and the truth is not in him. But whoever keeps His word, truly the love of God is perfected in him. By this we know that we are in Him. He who says he abides in Him ought himself also to walk just as He walked."

From time to time, it may seem impossible to live up to the teachings in the Bible. But, obeying God's commands are not burdensome. This does not mean that everything we do will be easy. Our personal feelings about his commands are irrelevant. In these verses, we can clearly see that we show our love for God by obeying him. In contrast, if we do not keep his commandments, then we do not really love him. Disobedience shows a lack of love.

We show our obedience and love for God by putting him first! "You shall love the Lord your God with all your heart, with all your soul, and with all your mind. This is the first and great commandment. And the second is like it: You shall love your neighbor as yourself. On these two commandments hang all the Law and the Prophets" (Matthew 22:37-40). Jesus makes the point that we should love God with everything we are and with everything we have. This demands that he be first in our lives. Truly, love for God must be a priority in our lives. He must come first.

We show our obedience and love for God by loving our brethren. "A new commandment I give unto you, that you love one another; as I have loved you that you also love one another. By this shall men know that you are my disciples if you have love one for another" (John 13:34-35). We are the only Bible some people ever experience and we must be prepared to extend Gods love to all. As Christians, we need to show the love we have for God every day, not just on occasion. By doing this, we demonstrate that God loves everyone just as they are. As a result, we advance the kingdom of God and allow his love to shine through us.

Lastly, we show our obedience and love for God by loving him enough to tell others about him! When you love someone, it's natural to want others to know about him or her. One who loves his parents will humbly tell others about them. Such is also true if we love God. "We cannot but speak the things we have seen and heard" (Acts 4:17-20). Surely we must remember the words of Christ; "Therefore, whoever confesses me before men, him I will also confess before my Father who is in heaven" (Matthew 10:32-33). Do you love God enough to tell others about him?

April

Chapter 4
Forgiveness

Forgiveness allows you to have peace within. It must be given freely, with no expectation in return. I believe forgiveness is a willful choice we make as Christians through a decision. In Colossians, the Bible compels us to forgive as the Lord has forgiven us. "Forbearing one another and forgiving one another if any man have a quarrel against any, even as Christ forgave you so also do ye" (Colossians 3:13).

Forgiveness is an act of faith, rooted in obedience to God. We must trust him to do the work in us required so that forgiveness will be completed. The scripture is clear in that, if we do not forgive, then we will not be forgiven; "For if ye forgive men their trespasses your heavenly father will also forgive you but if ye forgive not men their trespasses neither will your father forgive your trespasses" (Matthew 6:14-15).

As forgiveness is very important for us in our Christian walk, I created a few simple steps in to help you forgive. First, you must first have a desire to forgive. If there is no desire to forgive, chances are, forgiveness will not come and unforgiveness will remain. There are grave consequences for harboring unforgiveness. Unforgiveness opens the door of your heart to bitterness. Lingering heartaches from your past will ultimately create stress and strain in present and future relationships. Once you have the desire to forgive, forgiveness must be spoken. Whether you find yourself in the right or wrong, I believe you have to go to the person and express your hurt and forgiveness. By doing this, you will have peace within yourself. Finally, once forgiveness is spoken from a willing heart, it must be forgotten. The word 'forgotten' is defined as "No longer known; Dismissed from the mind." Some Christians are quick to say, "Oh, I forgive you," but still allow unforgiveness to occupy real estate in their minds. You must not allow yourself to dwell on past hurts.

Letting go of the past

About 8 years ago, a close family member killed my grandpa. This really hurt, as my grandfather was very dear to me. I could not believe that this person stole my grandfather's life. I don't like to use the word hate; however, I hated my grandpa's killer. I didn't want to forgive him, but not forgiving him began to negatively affect other areas of my life. When I surrendered my life over to God and began living His way, I learned to let go of my hatred toward this person. I realized that if I did not forgive, then my spiritual growth would be stunted. I wrote a letter to the person, stating I forgave and love him. About 2 days later, the person called and said thank you and expressed their love for me as well. This person also stated that it meant a lot to him that I forgave him. Not only did the person saying, "thank you" heal me; my spirit was touched by those words. I no longer have bad thoughts toward this person. Now, it is easier for me to forgive other people. In the end, each person must face God and be responsible for what they say and do.

Sometimes, hanging on to something is more painful than simply letting go. But in order for us to grow in our Christian walk, we need to let go of the past. Holding on to hurt only harms us. We must learn to let go in order to progress into who God wants us to be.

Oftentimes, letting go of the past requires letting go of people and things that no longer need to be a part of our lives. Certain relationships will hinder you from growing, and the lack of growth can cause you to miss out on the blessings of God. Let go and don't look back! Forgive, forget, and move on. God has better in store for you.

May

Chapter 5
Love

Nowadays, people throw love around far too much. They tell their partner, parents, and kids how much they love them, only to misuse, cheat, and even betray them. Love should be expressed with your whole heart. I must admit that I have hurt people that I claimed to love. I betrayed them. I now realize that one must know God in order to truly love, for God is love.

Most people are preoccupied with outward appearances, but God is concerned about our hearts. When you tell your parents or partner you love them, it must come from a genuine place deep inside. You must love others with your whole heart. I encourage you to make the decision to let the true love of God shine from within you. Love God and the people around you as you would want them to love you!

Examine Yourself

Take out a sheet of paper. On the right side of the paper, I would like you to write down all the positive things about yourself. On the left side of the paper, write down all of the negative things about yourself. Unfortunately, I bet you have written more negatives than positives. Let's change that today. Tear off that list of negatives and throw it away. Take the right side and keep it in a safe place so that you can look at it daily. A positive mind can lead to a powerful and positive life. When you truly change, then the love of God inside you will start to show, but you also must truly love yourself.

Love Yourself

You must first love yourself. Your beauty is not defined by your outward appearance. God has placed you on this Earth for a reason. God loves you. Put aside how you feel about yourself, and reach out to the one who is truly love-God. He will show you the beauty that is in you. While words can hurt, they can also heal. Look at yourself today and say, "I am somebody and I am special because I am made in the image of God." You are unique. You must stand strong as children of God, armed with the knowledge of who you are. Learn to love yourself first, and watch as happiness blossoms from within!

Message for all women

I am here to tell you that you are somebody and you are a beautiful human being created by God Himself. Don't allow any man to tear you down physically or emotionally. The first time a man places his hands on you abusively, walk away. I am here to tell you that you are never alone. There is a man that is loving, caring, honest, and will never leave you nor forsake you. His name is Jesus. Any man interested in a relationship with you should first have a relationship with Christ. A true man of God will love and respect you. Don't allow the pain and hurt to cause you to give up. God has greater things in store for you, so never feel sorry or get down on yourself. Stand up and be strong!

June

Chapter 6
Prayer

Prayer is extremely important because it is time spent in the presence of God. It is a time when we rid ourselves of our own desire and draw near to God. Although we can pray at any time, I feel that there are two times that are vital to Believers. We should seek God when we rise first thing in the morning. This is the time when we should thank God for another day and ask him to lead and guide us in truth. The second time is at the end of the day. As we review the events of the day, we should thank God for his mercy, confessing any wrongdoing, and seek God's forgiveness.

Prayer is powerful tool that can quickly change any situation. The moment we pray, is the moment we alter the environment around us. Prayer is a way to get closer to our father and we must not pray for ourselves but for other people also. Someone else's prayer could have spared you from destruction. No one can convince me that prayer does not work, because prayer saved my life.

I can remember a time when I was running late. I was so upset, but as I approached my destination, I noticed an accident ahead. At that moment, the spirit of the lord touched me and I knew that God caused the delay. My time spent in prayer earlier that day had changed the course of my life. I was so overcome with joy that I was brought to tears. I thank him with all my heart! Don't be anxious for anything. If you are in a hurry and running behind schedule, don't get upset. God could be redirecting your life. "Be anxious for nothing, but in everything by prayer and supplication, with thanksgiving, let your requests be made known to God; and the peace of God, which surpasses all understanding, will guard your hearts and minds through Christ Jesus" (Philippians 4:6-7). Stay faithful to him and pray, for you never know when a prayer could change a moment of a lifetime. God Bless!

July

Chapter 7
Marriage

Women, a wife does not find a husband, but when a man finds a wife he finds a good thing. A strong Godly marriage can withstand the test of times and will endure the storms of life. Nothing can sweep in and tear them apart, for they stand by each other and allow God to help and see them through. Husbands, your wife is a gift from God and should be treated as such. You must love, honor, and respect her at all times and not allow the little things separate your love. Women, if a man does not love God, then he will not be able to love you either. A man should have to go through God in order to gain your heart. Circumstances will change in a marriage, looks will change and that's when love will see all things through. During high times, low times, ups and downs, remember this too shall pass. Wives, remember to always build your husband up and never tear him down. Allow God to guide and lead your marriage and always keep one another in prayer! (Scriptures Hebrews 13:4, Mark 10:9 and

Genesis 2:24).

Although males and females are equal in relationship to Christ, the scriptures provide specific roles to each in marriage. The husband is to assume leadership in the home. This leadership should not be dictatorial, condescending, or patronizing to the wife, but should be in accordance with the example of Christ leading the church. "Husbands, love your wives, just as Christ loved the church.

Wives are to submit to the authority of their husbands. "Wives, submit to your husband, as is fitting in the Lord. Husbands love your wives and do not be harsh with them. Husbands, in the same way are considerate as you live with your wives, and treat them with respect.

In regard to the division of responsibilities in the home, the Bible instructs husbands to provide for their families. This means he works and makes enough money to sufficiently provide all the necessities of life for his wife and children. So, a man who makes no effort to provide for his family cannot rightly call himself a Christian. This does not mean that the wife cannot assist in supporting the family. Proverbs 31 demonstrates that a godly wife may surely do so, but providing for the family is not primarily her responsibility; it is her husband's. While a husband should help with the children and with household chores (thereby fulfilling his duty to love his wife), Proverbs 31 also makes it clear that the home is to be the woman's primary area of influence and responsibility. However, far too many women are stressed out and stretched to the breaking point. To prevent such stress, both husband and wife should prayerfully reorder their priorities and follow the Bibles instructions regarding their role. Conflicts regarding the division of labor in a marriage are bound to occur, but if both partners are submitted to Christ, these conflicts will be minimal. If a couple finds arguments over this issue are frequent, or if arguments seem to characterize the marriage, the problem is a spiritual one. In such an instance, the partners should recommit themselves to prayer and submission to Christ first, then to one another in an attitude of love and respect.

How to reconnect with your spouse's heart

Have that heart to heart connection. Sit with each other 10 minutes a day; hold each other hands and just talk. Ask caring and sincere questions. Get inside their heart and feel their emotion. Love each other more from the heart.

Ask them was there anything that happened today how their day was and how can you make tomorrow better. End the conversation with a loving and caring message. End the night in a positive way with no negative feelings. Negativity gives the enemy access to seek and destroy. Also take time and let your partner know the good in them, encourage, support, pray, and also read the word together for a family that prays together, stays together. Let them know you love them.

I encourage you to be positive and open with each other, as this will allow your hearts to grow together as one.

Love is Unconditional

Love is kind, caring, and honest. Love is not jealous but supportive and encouraging. Love is loving the person as they are. Love is faithfulness. Love is going that extra mile. True love is treating people like God treats us. If someone asked you why do you love your partner, what would you say?

Love knows the heart of another person, and if you can truly feel it, and you're willing to sacrifice your life for it, then that's love. Marriage shouldn't be taken lightly. Love does not leave when tragedy happens or walks out when times get tough. When you marry, you vow to love till' death. You must love your partner unconditionally. You will have ups and downs, but the marriages that usually last the longest are the ones that endure tests and trials! I pray that you experience this love. Allow God to guide and lead you into a lifetime of love and happiness.

August

Chapter 8
Chosen

God has called you, but it is up to you whether or not to accept and change or stay where you're at. In order to get something you've never had, you must be willing to do what you have never done. This world will certainly pass away. It will not be there with you when you come face to face with Jesus. You need to choose this day who you will serve. There are only two choices, Heaven or Hell. I know what the world of sin is like. I have been there myself and believe me what I have now being saved and living for God is more than I have ever had in the world. God never leaves you; he is always with you. Your friends, family, kids, may leave you, but He's never left you. God is waiting for you to come back. You have a gift, a destiny that needs to be fulfilled. God placed you here on Earth to bring glory to him. Stop sitting on your gift and use it for God's glory. His love for you never changes. His love never fails.

Direction

To get from one place to another you must follow the God's divine order. There are no shortcuts. You must follow his lead or else you will get off track. You cannot move ahead of him and his timing or you will miss out on a blessing. Stay strong and be patient. Allow God space to complete his work in his time.

Containment

If you continue to dwell in the past, you will never be able to grow in grace. The truth shall make you free, but if you don't pursue God's truth, you will remain stuck. Keep believing, praying, and trusting God. Stay consistent. Stop allowing yourself to be contained, because god wants you to have abundant life. God is faithful, so you must stand on his word every day, not on occasion. It takes time, faith, trust, and love! Don't allow yourself to shrink back into your comfort zone. Stretch out and press onward.

My friends and family know that I am extremely shy. When I committed my life to God, I was scared. Change is never easy, but I decided that I would complete whatever God required. I had to step out of my comfort zone. I was afraid to talk to people, let alone in front of a group of people. It's a scary feeling to stand up in front of a crowd. After six or seven months, I was requested to speak about forgiveness at my local church. I was scared and wanted to back out, but God spoke to me and said, "This isn't for you, there are people to hear what you have to say." In that moment, I knew I had to do it for God's glory. I have been called to help people. I certainly can't help people if I can't even speak to them. So, I overcame my fear and fulfilled my assignment.

Now, I talk to a lot of people that reach out to me. It's a great feeling to move forward in using my gift to help others. We can do all things through Christ. Before you were ever born, before the very foundation of the earth, God knew you. He chose you! He approved you and called you his own. People may have overlooked you in your life; maybe you were passed up for a job or overlooked by someone whose opinion you valued, but God won't ever overlook you! In fact, he handpicked you. He chose you to be holy and set you apart for himself. You are special. God has a purpose for your life. Reach out, grab it, and allow God to use you!

September

Chapter 9

Temptation

Life has many ups and downs. The world will always show you the pleasure of things, but never the consequences. The enemy will always show you the pleasure of the thing or situation. That's how the enemy baits you into sin. Actions have consequences. What we do can and will affect others. Just because you can do something doesn't mean it's a good idea, and it doesn't mean you are removed from the chain of cause and effect. It is easy to be tempted, and yes, it will be hard. But when you stand on the word of God, resisting temptation becomes easier. You must trust God to see it through and not allow the enemy to trick you.

Seek and Destroy

The enemy comes only to steal, kill, and destroy. During these trying times, your faith must stand strong and allow God to see you through. We must walk by faith and not by sight, for what we see is only temporary. The enemy will come through different avenues and areas in your life, such as your mind, family friends, kids, and even your workplace. The enemy first attack is always aimed at the mind. He aims to seeds of doubt. He knows what your weaknesses are in your life. Next, the enemy will use those closest to you, mainly family and friends. Some of your friends and family may not be saved and enemy will use that relationship to lure back to places God has delivered you from. You must stand under the blood of Jesus and trust that He will see you through. When you stand strong in your faith, you can avoid temptation. The enemy may even try use your own children to test you, but you must remain faithful and obedient in all things. Finally, you may be tempted in your workplace. You should never compromise your integrity to "fit in." Talk is cheap. If we claim that we are saved, then we must live it every day, not just when we feel like it. I encourage you to remain faithful and allow God to lead. Don't allow the enemy to come and destroy what God has brought together. You didn't come this far to give up now. Stay strong.

October

Chapter 10

Which Will You Choose? Heaven or Hell

Time is running out. While no man knows the day and the hour of the Lord's return, I believe that we are in the season of his coming. Is this the time to worry, and run from God? No. We should turn to God now more than ever. We must open our eyes and realize what's happening in the world.

As we see the signs of earthquakes, tornados, birds falling from the sky, rising food and gas prices and increased crime, this should cause us to wake up. What more does God have to show for us to realize that the son is soon to return? Now is the time to repent and ask God into your heart.

I ask that you please pray, get into the word, and ask for forgiveness before it is too late. Seek him now. God arms are open to receive you with the love. He is reaching out and you need to grab hold of his love today. God will meet you right where you are. God loves you whether you realize it or not. I pray that you ask God into your heart and get into a church.

Heaven or Hell

If Jesus returned today, where would you spend eternity? This is a serious question that must be answered honestly.

This earth is coming to an end. You will spend your eternity in Heaven or Hell. Hell is a place you don't want to go. What you do here on earth affects where you go in the end. Will you walk with God and live his way or will you walk the world and live the enemy's way?

Heaven is a place where you live eternally with God, Jesus, and your loved ones. It is a place without pain, hurt, sorrow, and tears; a place of nothing but love. Isn't this a place you would love to be forever? Isn't this a place where you would love to be? Now, imagine the worst place in the world, completely dark and void of peace. Imagine a place of suffering and eternal torment. Forever is a long time. Can you handle this pain and torture forever? Are you having fun living in the world? Are you living for God or are you living for yourself? Don't let the temporary pleasures of this world deceive you. There is no future in drinking, drugs, clubs, and smoking, lusting, cheating, lying and killing. What will you say when stand-alone before God's judgment? You will not be able to defend your actions to God. You can only serve one Master; you're either going to serve the world or you are going to serve God. What can the world give you that is greater than God? My answer is nothing. Your actions will ultimately determine where you spend eternity. Fortunately, God gives you a chance every day to change your life and you can start right now. His mercies are new every morning. Repeat after me, "Lord Jesus I ask for you to come into my heart forgive me of my sin. I believe that you died on the cross for my salvation. Today, I make you my Lord and savior. Amen." If you said this prayer with all your heart, I believe God has entered into your heart and you are now saved. I ask that you attend a church, read the Bible, and pray for God's direction. Be blessed.

November

Chapter 11

Giving Thanks, Helping Others

Giving God the Glory for all Things

We should be thankful in all things, no matter how big or small. People are all too quick to take credit for their own success, when God is responsible for making provision for us. When you stay faithful and obedient, he will remain faithful to you and shower you with blessings. So the next time you're running late, find that check you weren't expecting in the mail, or get approved for a loan that you don't qualify for, stop and give thanks to God. He deserves the glory for leading and guiding you in the right places and time.

We should be thankful in any situation we find ourselves, whether it be good or bad. Being thankful in difficult times allows you to see the greatness of God. When the storm is over, your tribulations will become powerful testimonies, which will allow you to comfort and encourage others in times of despair. You may not have arrived to the place you desire, but be thankful you are no longer in the place you were. Be thankful for all things.

A new day of life, a roof over your head, kids, family, friends, being saved, or job are all reasons to give thanks to God. As you look back throughout your life, I am sure you can find many blessings, both great and small. So as you celebrate thanksgiving this year, be thankful. "Make thankfulness your sacrifice to God and keep the vows you made to the Most High" (Psalms 50:14).

Helping Others

Find someone to help today and every day; be a blessing. When you give to those in need, you bless God. And he knows how to repay you back! "He who is gracious to a poor man lends to the Lord, and He will repay him for his good deed" (Proverbs 19:17). You may not be able to give money, but you can babysit for a single mother. Why don't you give her a break? Tell her, "You do something special for yourself. Here's a gift certificate. Go enjoy yourself at the mall. We will keep your children tonight." If you notice one of your friends wearing the same clothes all the time, why don't you step up to the plate and say, "Take this gift certificate and go get yourself some new clothes." You're never more like God, than when you do something to bless someone else. Be a blessing, whether great or small. Learn to be good to people in your everyday walk. When you stop to get a cup of coffee at work, bring your coworker back a cup too. When traffic backs up on the freeway, let other cars merge into your lane. When in the store and you have a lot of items, but the person behind you only has a little, let them go first. Remember, true love is always followed by action. People are watching us, and one of the best witnesses we can have is simply by being good to people. God will meet your own needs as you meet the needs of others. Jesus said, "When you do it to the least of one of these, its like you're doing it unto Me," (Matt 25:40).

December

Chapter 12

Reason for the Season

Gift of the Season

During this Christmas season remember the giver of the gift of life. Christmas is not about Santa or how many gifts you can buy. Remember be grateful with what you currently have. Whether it is a husband, wife, children, home, food on the table or simply being able to enjoy another day of life, be thankful. Remember the reason for which this season is celebrated. Remember the gift which was given to us, namely Jesus! So during this holiday season, celebrate the love of Jesus and his sacrifice for you!

When I was living in sin, I was constantly depressed and unhappy. The enemy doesn't care whether you live or die. I believed I was worthless and that I would never find happiness in life. I was so convinced of this lie that I attempted to end my own life at ages 14 and 17. But God spared my life. God decided that it was not time for me to leave this earth, because I had not fulfilled his will for my life. After 14 years of tests and trials, my life has turned the corner. I currently write the newsletter for my church and also leave inspirational messages for people. When you surrender your life to God, you will never feel depressed or unhappy again. Once you experience God's love, you will never feel or look the same again. God is good. He saved me and my husband at the same time. He saved our marriage, blessed us with a new home, a new car, and a great job for my husband all within one year of us dedicating our lives to him. However, the greatest gift waits for us at the end of this life. One day we will spend eternity in his presence. I know God has more great things in store for me and I will continue to do his will and give him the glory! So I ask you today, if you are someone that is not saved and so tired of things being the same, repent and be saved. Connect with a local church and watch the greatness of God!!! Be blessed for you are blessed!

Final Thoughts

When you change the way you look at things, the things you look at will change. If your presence doesn't make an impact, your absence won't make a difference. You may feel overlooked, but God always sees the best that is within. People can hurt you even without saying a word. Trust that God will see you through. When you die, the life you lived will speak for you. What will people remember you by? You can't live a devil and die an angel. If you judge people, you have no time to love them. No matter how big or small the blessing, always give God the glory!

www.ingramcontent.com/pod-product-compliance
Lightning Source LLC
Chambersburg PA
CBHW060218050426
42446CB00013B/3106